Hello

Thank you for picking up this little book. We
hope you enjoy it!

The veterinary profession is very special. It
is full of people who genuinely care and want
to do the right thing for their patients and
owners. We know it can be tough and requires
hard work, commitment, and kindness.

This book is a token of our thanks to the
wonderful veterinary teams, and a reminder of
how great you really are!

With warm wishes from
the whole team at VetCT

VetCT provides specialist support to vets around the world. Our values
are based around kindness and care, and our mission is to help every
vet feel their best and be their best every day. We created the VetCT
App to connect you with our team of friendly specialists, 24/7, for
advice and support whenever you need it.

To find out more visit www.vet-ct.com or scan me

We all need a reminder of how
brilliant we actually are, now and
again.

VETCT

Clinical support in your pocket

Some days clients can seem demanding,
and we can feel like we are spinning
plates....

...

Or maybe we seem to have projects
coming out of our ears...

Sometimes that pesky critic appears on
our shoulder to tell us about
everything that we've 'missed' and where
we should have done better.

..or from time to time you might feel like a
fraud.
(pssst.. you're not).

Here's your reminder that you ARE
valuable.
And amazing.
And brilliant.
Someone wants to let you know that
today.

You're an awesome life-saving,
anal-gland dodging, anaesthetising,
multi-tasking, vet nurse hero.
Or maybe you're a teaching hero, an
equine hero, a referral hero, exotics
hero or an industry hero.
You see, vet nurse heroes come in
many guises.
Not doing a nurse clinic for a few
years doesn't make you any less of a
hero.
Neither does having never done a
scale and polish.
You have your own unique set of
experiences, that will never be the
same as anyone else's.

Sometimes we forget about that uniqueness.

We are often quick to see our peers post online about their triumphs yet not credit our own zone of genius.

We spot those 'less' experienced gaining further qualifications, yet forget they'd be envious of our ninja skills from years in practice.

Eleanor Roosevelt said "comparison is the thief of joy" and oh boy was she right.

The odds of a human being born were calculated at 1 in 400 trillion.

Wow.

You're the only you on Earth, you just happen to be a vet nurse too.

You're totally unique (and valuable). How special is that?

You can't compare unique, so why bother trying?

In this uniqueness are some amazing
strengths and qualities.
Sometimes we forget those too.
The person who sent you this book can
see them all too well.
Realign with your strengths, spend some
time to soak up your triumphs (of which
there are plenty).
There are thousands of animal lives
that have changed because of you.
Be kind to yourself.

How can we be kind to ourselves?
Let's remember we don't have to
believe that inner critic.
You didn't choose those beliefs it
tells you.
You're not a fraud (unless you
bought your RVN badge from a
stranger...which you didn't).

VETCT
Clinical support in your pocket

And what else?
Nourish yourself.
Set time aside for this amazing vet nurse
to recharge.
Find what works for you.
Mindfulness or meditation?
Maybe you're a yogi, or a runner.
Perhaps you're a crafter.
What if you're an adrenaline junkie?
Or a skier, or even part of a Mexican band?
Perhaps adding a weekly massage is a must.
For some that might include medications or
therapy.
You do you.

On the topic of being kind, let's be
kind to each other too.
Make the extra cuppa.
Check in with your colleagues.
Let's not judge, and try to see other's
perspective too.
We never know what's going on for
anyone else.
Let's be one big team, with everyone a
unique and valuable member.
#bekind (always)

It's ok not to know something.... at any stage in your vet nurse journey.
SVNs are allowed not to know things, as are those thirty years out.
Let's remember we work in teams and are here to help each other build our knowledge.

Equally, failing doesn't make you a failure.
At the times of failure, we often have our greatest lessons.
Ask: what can I learn from this?
What would your best friend say to you?
Let's start speaking to ourselves in that way too.

Sometimes being kind to ourselves is
asking for help.
This might be for work, for home life or
when we don't feel ourselves.
We are superheroes, but even Superman was
Clark Kent for some of the day.
You don't have to know everything, nobody
does.
Reach out - no vet nurse is an island.

VETCT
Clinical support in your pocket

www.katiefordvet.com

We are the master of our ship, the captain
of our fate*.
(*but we don't have to sail alone)

The email saying you secretly failed
your finals is NOT on its way.

You earned your qualification, it was
not by mistake.

70% of the population have
experienced feeling like an
imposter.... we simply can't all be
frauds.
Not even you*.
(*or you!)

VETCT
Clinical support in your pocket

Some days will be tricky.
Some days we will be pulled in 87
different directions (and the vet will
have your pen again!).
But keep your focus on what matters.
Find joy in the small things.
The puppies, the foals, the calves.
The thank you cards and messages.
The laughs with your colleagues.
The differences that you make every
day.
Find time for gratitude.
Find time for you too.

Thank you
Awesome
Vet Nurse

Whilst we're on the topic of thanks.
Accept the compliments.
Try to stop the "yeah, but"s.
The thanks is justified, even as part of
a team, you can share with them too, but
soak up your contribution.
It's their thanks to give, they made that
decision, receive it graciously.

The ones who complain and say things
they'd later regret - let's not give our
power to them.
None of us ever know the full story.
Maybe they had a bad day too.
This doesn't excuse it, but might
explain it.
We're all human.
We're sorry for the things people said
that they probably don't mean.
Let's keep coming back to kindness.

There are so many people out there
that are grateful for the differences
that you've made.
The animals you've hand-fed.
The students you've taught.
The owners that you've been a kind,
listening ear for.
The diet advice you've given..
The people you've helped in difficult
times.
Remember those ones, they definitely
remember you.

VETCT

Clinical support in your pocket

Ask yourself: what went well today?
Be your own cheerleader, look for the
good.
It might seem tricky at first, but
give it a try.
Give yourself some credit, you
deserve it.
Lots of people think that you do.

And whilst we are talking about
credit….
There was once a time you doubted you'd
ever be a vet nurse.
You did it.
There was a time you doubted you'd pass
your OSCEs or exams.
You did it.

You are so full of potential to grow,
but you're still valuable all the same.

You do so many amazing things every
day that you might take for granted.
You have impacted so many lives,
human and animal.
You are a skilled vet nursing ninja.
Small animal or equine.
First opinion or referral.
Coaching or lecturing.
Industry or public health.
SVN or RVN.
This remains true.
Soak that up.

Sometimes the Sunday Scaries rear
their head.
"What if there's been a disaster over
the weekend?"
"What if I've made a mistake?"
"What if Monday throws me something
I can't handle?"
Change the 'what if' to 'even if'.
Even if you've made a mistake, you'll
learn something.
Even if you don't know what to do,
someone else will.

From time to time you won't have a clue
what to do.
That's ok.
You're not a bad vet nurse.
Someone else will know… reach out.
Speak with your team.
Have faith in your skill set too.
Reflect back and give yourself some
credit when you overcome the obstacle,
even with help.
This is where we grow.

You're also not a bad vet nurse if you
step out of clinical work.
Or because you return to it.
Nor if you move to referral, or step
into academia.
Be you in public health, industry,
practice, teaching or referral, you are
valuable.
You're also not a bad human being if
you change your mind and want to fish
for a living instead.

You're valuable.
Not because of the letters after your
name, however many there may be.
Or because of where you work.
Or because of your social media
following, or the extra certificates
that you have.
Nor does your value rest on your case
outcomes, or whether you can do a
tricky task solo.
Plenty of people think you're
valuable...
....just because you're you*.

(*even on the days where you don't get out from under
the duvet and watch TV all day)

And don't forget that being you involves so much more than your job title.

You're a son or a daughter, and maybe a sibling, a cousin, perhaps a mother or a father.

There are many facets to you.

You'll have your own set of things that make you happy.

Always remember to embrace those things.

You're allowed happiness, and not on a delayed payment plan.

Spend time on all of you, as well as your career.

Nobody ever says they regret not working enough.

Look after that amazing person.
Be kind to yourself.
You cannot pour from an empty
cup.
You're allowed to stop and have
a break.
In fact, we suggest you go and
pour yourself a brew.
Grab a biscuit too if you like.

So this has been your reminder:
You are an amazing, unique, valuable
human being that has their own
individual journey, who just happens
to be a brilliant vet nurse too.
Remember that.

About the
author

This little book was brought to you by
Dr. Katie Ford, a veterinary surgeon, speaker
and coach. Katie had her own journey with
self-doubt and imposter syndrome as a vet,
despite externally looking like a success.
She's passionate about helping others to
believe in themselves and their value, and
realise it is independent of qualifications
and external things.

You can read more about Katie at
www.katiefordvet.com.
@katiefordvet

This book was gifted to you by
VetCT.
To find out more visit
www.vet-ct.com
or scan me

VETCT
Clinical support in your pocket

A book of reminders for a brilliant vet nurse.

by Katie Ford

www.katiefordvet.com

Printed in Great Britain
by Amazon